THE STORY OF THE
DALLAS COWBOYS

NFL TODAY

THE STORY OF THE DALLAS COWBOYS

SCOTT CAFFREY

CREATIVE PAPER BACKS

Cover: Defensive tackle Bob Lilly (top), tight end
Martellus Bennett (bottom)
Page 2: Linebacker Lee Roy Jordan
Pages 4–5: Defensive end Chris Canty
Pages 6–7: Quarterback Tony Romo

....

Published by Creative Paperbacks
P.O. Box 227, Mankato, Minnesota 56002
Creative Paperbacks is an imprint of
The Creative Company
www.thecreativecompany.us

Design and production by Blue Design
Design Associate: Sarah Yakawonis
Printed in the United States of America

Photographs by Corbis (Bettmann, Tom Fox/
Dallas Morning News, Dana Hoff, James D. Smith/
Icon SMI, Irwin Thompson/Dallas Morning News),
Getty Images (Jonathan Daniel, Diamond Images,
Focus On Sport, George Gojkovich, Wesley Hitt,
Paul Jasienski, Hunter Martin, Ronald Martinez,
Al Messerschmidt, Al Messerschmidt/NFL, George
Rose, Tony Tomsic/NFL, Greg Trott/NFL Photos)

The Library of Congress has cataloged the
hardcover edition as follows:

Caffrey, Scott.
The story of the Dallas Cowboys / by Scott Caffrey.
p. cm. — (NFL today)
Includes index.
ISBN 978-1-58341-753-9 (hardcover)
ISBN 978-0-89812-534-4 (pbk)
1. Dallas Cowboys (Football team)—History—
Juvenile literature. I. Title. II. Series.

GV956.D3C34 2008
796.332'64097642812—dc22   2008022684

First Edition
9 8 7 6 5 4 3 2 1

CONTENTS

ON THE SIDELINES

MEET THE COWBOYS

THE LITTLE TEAM ON THE PRAIRIE

X- -

X The Dallas area is today home to professional teams in all four major sports (football, baseball, basketball, and hockey), but none are more famous or beloved than the Cowboys.

Gleaming brightly from the vast Texas prairie along the Trinity River is the city of Dallas. The Texas metropolis is thought to be named after George Mifflin Dallas, who was vice president of the United States when the city was founded in 1846. Dallas is the heart of Texas's oil and cotton industries, which helped it to rise to prominence as the state's second-largest city.

Texas has a long-standing and passionate football tradition, and Dallas lies at the heart of it. While high school football is a treasured Friday night custom, college football is equally popular. Each year, the city hosts the Red River Shootout between the University of Texas and the University of Oklahoma. But since 1960, residents of the "Lone Star State" have perhaps cheered most passionately for the team with the lone star on its helmets—the Dallas Cowboys.

The Cowboys were born of a rivalry between two leagues. In 1959, after repeatedly being denied a new franchise by the National Football League (NFL), Dallas millionaire Lamar Hunt retaliated by starting the American Football League (AFL) with seven other owners. Hunt's flagship team was the Dallas Texans.

To compete with the newly formed rival, the NFL awarded an expansion team to another Dallas millionaire, Clint Murchison Jr. In 1959, Murchison's team had not yet been formally admitted to the NFL. But that didn't stop him from making his first important hiring—general manager Tex Schramm, who had previously held the same position with the Los Angeles Rams. Schramm's first office was a borrowed desk in a corner of the Texas Auto Club. "People would crowd in there to map routes for trips, and I'd be over in a corner discussing player contracts on the phone," Schramm remembered. "Sometimes they'd listen in. The noise was unbelievable."

From these humble beginnings, Murchison, Schramm, and chief scout Gil Brandt set out to build a team. Because they couldn't name a head coach before being awarded official franchise status, they signed former New York Giants assistant and Texas native Tom Landry to a "personal services" contract. "People were calling him a young genius for what he had done with the Giants' defense," Schramm later said. "He was the only person I actually ever talked to about the job."

Schramm also had the difficult task of assembling players for an unofficial team. So, determined to acquire a quality quarterback, he got creative. His top choice was a two-

TEX SCHRAMM

PRESIDENT, GENERAL MANAGER
COWBOYS SEASONS: 1959-89

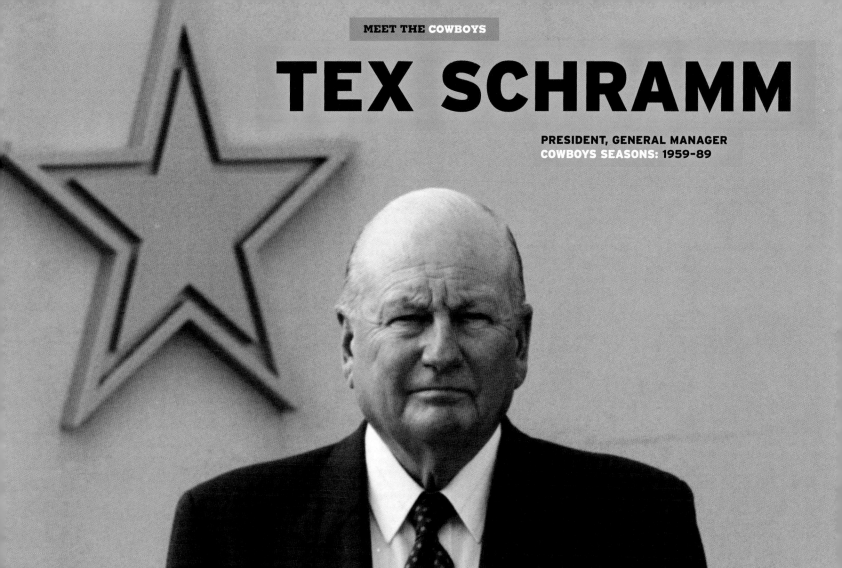

Tex Schramm was the first architect of the Cowboys. But many of Schramm's innovations extended far beyond Dallas. Some ideas, such as dancing cheerleaders, were so popular that other teams adopted them. Other ideas became such league-changing concepts that Schramm has been credited with almost single-handedly altering major aspects of the game. For example, while setting hash marks in the center of the field and giving the referee a microphone is taken for granted these days, they were major advancements when Schramm suggested them in the 1970s. Creating instant replay, implementing sudden-death overtime, and expanding the Wild Card playoff system are just some of the other ideas Schramm developed for the ever-evolving league. One of Schramm's main areas of focus, however, was player safety. Between 1974 and 1979, he lobbied to move the goalposts from the goal line to the end line, to ban helmet-slapping by defensive linemen, and to create the "in-the-grasp" rule to protect quarterbacks from injury. Schramm's reputation was so exemplary that he was named president of the World League of American Football when the NFL first tried to make itself an international sport in 1989.

THE FIRST TEXANS

Texas's first professional football franchise, the Dallas Texans, barely lasted a full season in 1952. The team began with high hopes, as owner Giles Miller figured Texas—a huge state with a long-standing reputation for great high school and college football—would be a perfect fit for a pro football franchise. "There is room enough in Texas for all kinds of football," Miller declared. But the 1952 Texans barely got off the ground and never approached a win. No wins also meant no fans. Miller lost so much money so quickly that he was unable to meet payroll. So, rather than stick it out and hope for a turnaround, he cut his losses early and returned his team to the league with five games left in the season. The league transferred the Texans to Hershey, Pennsylvania, and made them a road team. The gimmick worked, as the Texans finally got a win on Thanksgiving Day against the Chicago Bears. It would be another eight years before residents of the Lone Star State could cheer for another hometown professional football team.

time All-American named "Dandy" Don Meredith from local Southern Methodist University. Using cloak-and-dagger tactics, Schramm asked his old friend George Halas, owner of the Chicago Bears, for help in making the deal. Halas drafted Meredith and promptly traded him to Dallas. Schramm used a similar tactic to sign running back Don Perkins.

F inally, on January 28, 1960, the Dallas Cowboys were officially admitted into the NFL. At 35, Landry became the league's youngest head coach. Drawn from a "player pool" of other teams' leftovers, many of the first Cowboys didn't last, but linebacker Jerry Tubbs and receiver Frank Clarke would eventually become stars. Veteran quarterback Eddie LeBaron was brought in to start while Meredith adjusted to the pro game. The best the Cowboys could do that first season was a tie with the Giants, finishing the year 0–11–1.

The Cowboys finally got on the winning side of some games the next two seasons, going 4–9–1 and 5–8–1. But the momentum waned in 1962, and the Cowboys could only watch as their crosstown rivals, the Texans, won the AFL championship over the two-time defending champion Houston Oilers. Still, the Cowboys believed they were on the right track. "Virtually everybody in the organization had a drive to win, and they were loyal," Schramm said. That

attitude became a hallmark that solidified the team. As competition for fans became too difficult for the Dallas Texans, Hunt moved his team to Kansas City in 1963 and renamed it the Chiefs. Dallas now belonged exclusively to the Cowboys.

X From 1962 until 1968, the Cowboys were led on the field by quarterback Don Meredith and from the sidelines by coach Tom Landry.

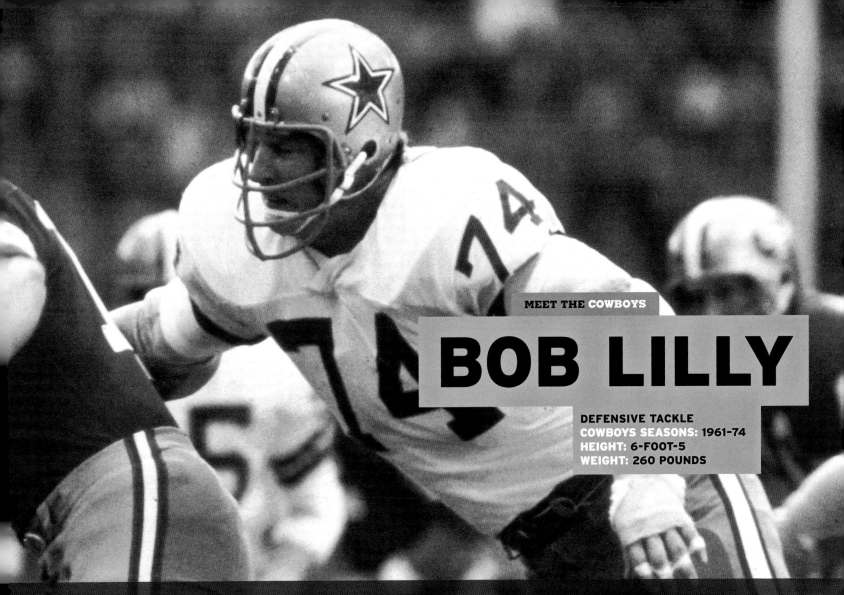

BOB LILLY

DEFENSIVE TACKLE
COWBOYS SEASONS: 1961-74
HEIGHT: 6-FOOT-5
WEIGHT: 260 POUNDS

It's no wonder Bob Lilly was nicknamed "Mr. Cowboy." Nearly everything he did was a Cowboys first—first draft pick, first multitime All-Pro selection, first name inducted into the team's Ring of Honor, and first Pro Football Hall of Fame inductee. The Cowboys don't retire jersey numbers, but no player has ever worn number 74 in Dallas since Lilly retired in 1974. Armed with a rare combination of durability and skill, Lilly had exceptional field vision, catlike reflexes, and enough strength to fight through constant double- and triple-teams. And he never missed a game in his 14-year career. "I didn't think a man that big could be so quick," Miami Dolphins guard Bob Kuechenberg said. A change of position in 1971 would alter the course of Lilly's career—and the Cowboys' fortunes—for the better. When coach Tom Landry moved Lilly from his normal defensive end position to the interior as a tackle, the famed "Doomsday Defense" suddenly had its engine. And the Cowboys went from Super Bowl losers to champions in one year.

THE COWBOYS SADDLE UP

While Meredith and Perkins were poised to lead the Cowboys' offense, tackle Bob Lilly was ready to lead the defense. Dallas had selected the fast and powerful pass rusher with its first-ever draft choice in 1961. Lilly would go on to become one of the greatest defensive tackles in NFL history, playing in 11 Pro Bowls and becoming the first Cowboys star inducted into the Pro Football Hall of Fame. "A man like that comes along once in a lifetime," said Coach Landry. "He is something a little bit more than great. Nobody is better than Bob Lilly."

The Cowboys continued to build around Lilly by drafting defensive talent such as linebacker Lee Roy Jordan in 1963. The next season was particularly important to the team's growth, as Dallas welcomed ballhawking safety Mel Renfro and wide receiver "Bullet" Bob Hayes, a world-class sprinter. Dallas also took a chance by drafting Heisman Trophy-winning quarterback Roger Staubach from the U.S. Naval Academy, even though he wouldn't be able to play right away because of his four-year service commitment to the navy.

In 1966, Dallas went 10–3–1 and made the playoffs for the first time. Over the next four seasons, the Cowboys would ride high, posting a combined 42–13–1 record. In 1966 and 1967, the young team in silver and blue charged all the way to the NFL Championship Game, losing to the mighty Green Bay Packers both times.

The 1967 championship game in Green Bay was a classic. Played in extraordinarily frigid conditions, it is remembered today as the "Ice Bowl." The official game-time temperature was -13 degrees, with a windchill around -48. The cold overwhelmed Lambeau Field's turf heating system, which turned the field into a rock-hard sheet of ice. It also overwhelmed some players. Hayes, for example, inadvertently gave the Packers defense a sign. When he wasn't the intended receiver on a play, he put his cold hands in his pants to keep warm. When Hayes was the intended target, he lined up normally with his hands out. After keying in on this, the Packers were able to shut down the Cowboys' passing offense. The game ended when legendary Packers quarterback Bart Starr scored on a quarterback sneak to hand Dallas a bitter 21–17 defeat. "I was just happy to get out of that game alive," Lilly said. "I'll never forget that game."

After coming close to a championship twice, the Cowboys

X Don Meredith and the Cowboys came back from a 14–0 deficit to go ahead in the "Ice Bowl" but could not hold a fourth-quarter lead.

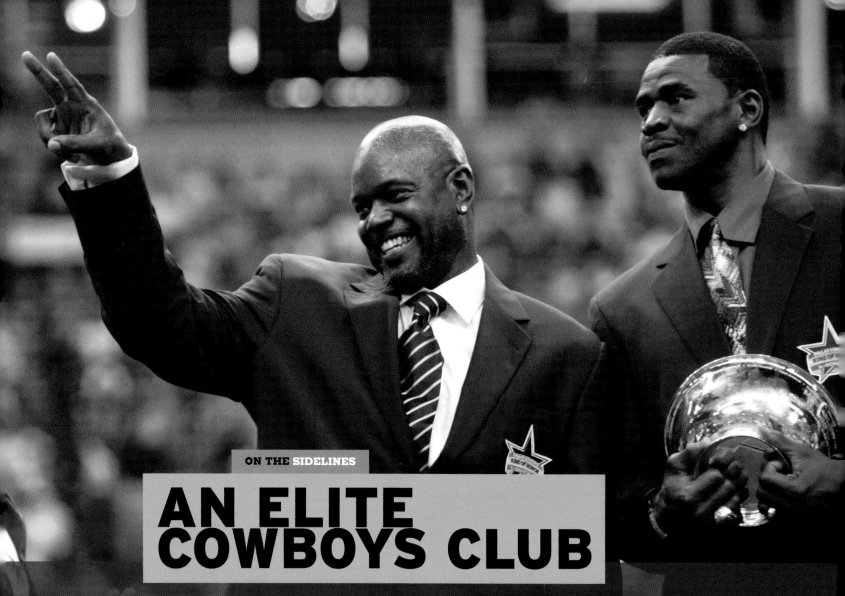

ON THE SIDELINES

AN ELITE COWBOYS CLUB

Created by Tex Schramm and unveiled on "Bob Lilly Day" (November 23, 1975), the Dallas Cowboys' Ring of Honor acknowledges those people who have made outstanding contributions to the franchise. By 2008, 17 Cowboys had been so honored, their names and years of service displayed in silver around the middle rim of Texas Stadium. Ring of Honor inductees were chosen by a committee of one: first it was Schramm, and from 1989 onward, it was team owner Jerry Jones. Schramm's first choices were all men of great personal character: Bob Lilly, Don Meredith, Don Perkins, Chuck Howley, Mel Renfro, and Roger Staubach. Later inductees followed the same precedent and included Tony Dorsett, Bob Hayes, Lee Roy Jordan, Randy White, safety Cliff Harris, offensive tackle Rayfield Wright, Tom Landry, and the Ring's originator himself, Tex Schramm. In 2005, three former players were simultaneously inducted during halftime ceremonies of a Monday Night Football game. Known collectively as "The Triplets," Troy Aikman, Emmitt Smith (pictured, left), and Michael Irvin (pictured, right) were major offensive cogs for Dallas's three-time Super Bowl championship teams of the '90s.

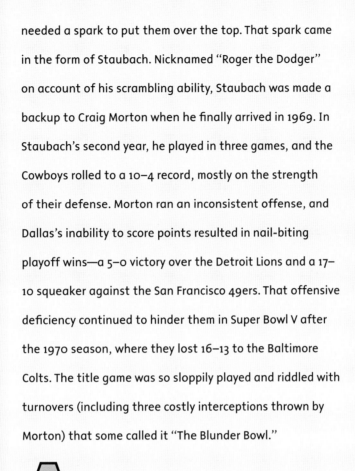

needed a spark to put them over the top. That spark came in the form of Staubach. Nicknamed "Roger the Dodger" on account of his scrambling ability, Staubach was made a backup to Craig Morton when he finally arrived in 1969. In Staubach's second year, he played in three games, and the Cowboys rolled to a 10–4 record, mostly on the strength of their defense. Morton ran an inconsistent offense, and Dallas's inability to score points resulted in nail-biting playoff wins—a 5–0 victory over the Detroit Lions and a 17–10 squeaker against the San Francisco 49ers. That offensive deficiency continued to hinder them in Super Bowl V after the 1970 season, where they lost 16–13 to the Baltimore Colts. The title game was so sloppily played and riddled with turnovers (including three costly interceptions thrown by Morton) that some called it "The Blunder Bowl."

As proof of just how great the Cowboys defense was, linebacker Chuck Howley became the only player of a losing team ever to be voted the Super Bowl's Most Valuable Player (MVP). A consummate professional and dedicated teammate, Howley was grateful for the honor but dismayed by the loss. "The award is tremendous," he said. "But I wish it was the world championship. They go hand in hand."

AMERICA'S TEAM

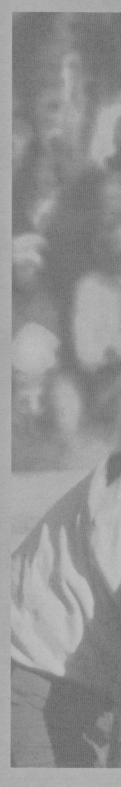

The Cowboys put the painful loss behind them and came roaring back in 1971 with Staubach installed as the full-time starter. The defense led the way again, but the offense began to develop some punch with young running back Duane Thomas and veteran recevier Lance Alworth. With all cylinders finally firing, Dallas marched to New Orleans for Super Bowl VI, where it put on a dominating performance against the Miami Dolphins.

Dallas's defense limited Miami to 185 yards of total offense and just 3 points, and Staubach claimed MVP honors by efficiently picking apart the Dolphins' defense with long scoring drives. After more than a decade of close calls, Dallas had its first world championship with a decisive 24–3 conquest. "My most satisfying moment as a professional was in that locker room in New Orleans," Staubach later said. "Dallas had been a winning team but until that moment had the reputation of not being able to win the big one. I looked around that locker room at Bob Lilly, Chuck Howley, and the

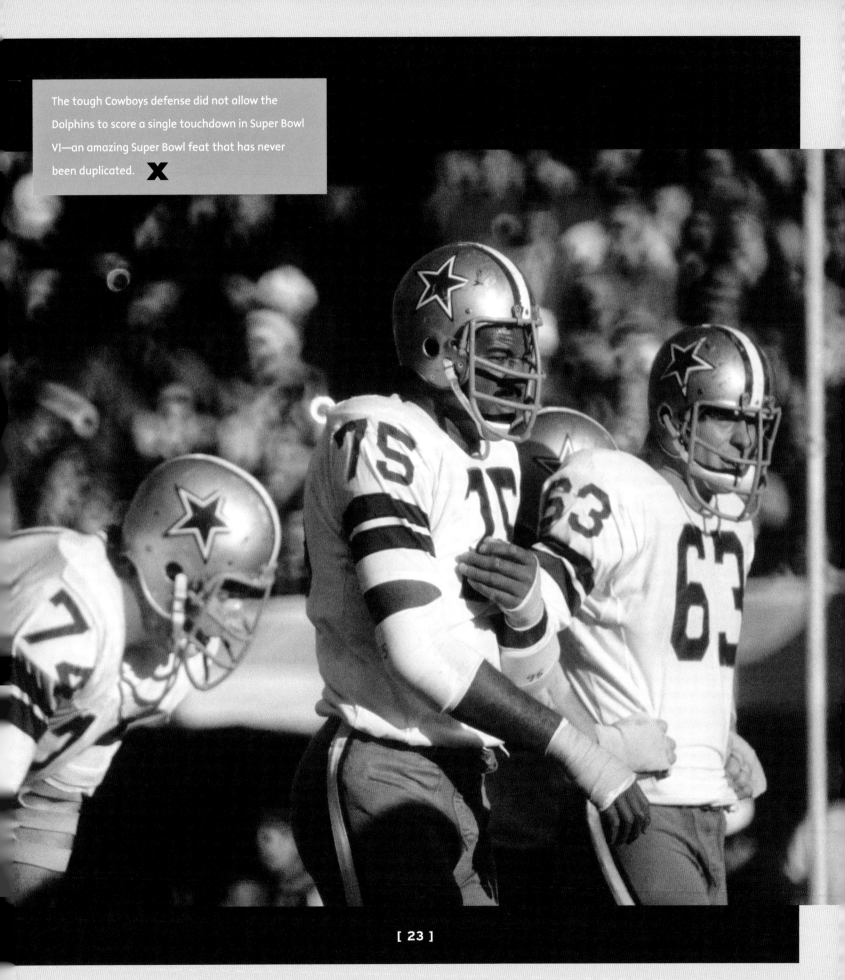

The tough Cowboys defense did not allow the Dolphins to score a single touchdown in Super Bowl VI—an amazing Super Bowl feat that has never been duplicated. **X**

MEET THE COWBOYS

ROGER STAUBACH

QUARTERBACK
COWBOYS SEASONS: 1969-79
HEIGHT: 6-FOOT-3
WEIGHT: 197 POUNDS

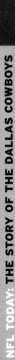

NFL TODAY: THE STORY OF THE DALLAS COWBOYS

Roger Staubach's story is one of patience. After being drafted in 1964, Staubach first had to serve his four-year commitment to the U.S. Navy. Then, after arriving in Dallas as a 27-year-old rookie in 1969, he waited even longer behind starter Craig Morton. Finally, in 1971, Staubach began his takeover in a game against the Chicago Bears when coach Tom Landry experimented with "musical quarterbacks," alternating Staubach and Morton on each first down and sometimes on each play. Although Dallas lost, the offense gained more than 500 yards. After that, Landry had enough faith in Staubach to hand him the offensive reins for good, and the quarterback reeled off 10 consecutive wins, including the Cowboys' first Super Bowl victory. Staubach was a smart quarterback who never panicked when the Cowboys were losing. "You could never defeat Roger mentally or physically," Landry said. "He was like that in a game, in practice, or in the business world." Indeed, Staubach engineered 23 fourth-quarter come-from-behind victories during his career. That confidence, and his knack for winning, earned "Roger the Dodger" another nickname: "Captain Comeback."

[24]

other veterans. I could see the pride on their faces. It was a great feeling."

After posting back-to-back 10–4 seasons that ended in National Football Conference (NFC) Championship Game losses (the AFL had merged with the NFL in 1970, creating the National and American Conferences), 1974 was the first time in nearly a decade that Dallas did not make the postseason. But in 1976, the Cowboys made a determined charge back to Super Bowl X. Facing the Pittsburgh Steelers, Dallas lost 21–17 in a game that came down to the wire. Despite these big-game losses, the Cowboys' amazing run of success gained them fans throughout the country and earned them the lasting nickname of "America's Team."

In 1977, a new star arrived in Dallas: Heisman Trophy-winning running back Tony Dorsett, who added an exciting new dimension to the Cowboys' offense. After racking up 12 touchdowns, rushing for 1,007 yards, and lifting the Cowboys back to the top of the NFC East Division, Dorsett earned the NFL Offensive Rookie of the Year award. Over the next 7 years, Dorsett would rush for more than 1,000 yards each season, with only a players' strike in 1982 interrupting the streak. In a Monday Night Football game in 1983, he made a spectacular 99-yard romp against the Minnesota Vikings that will always

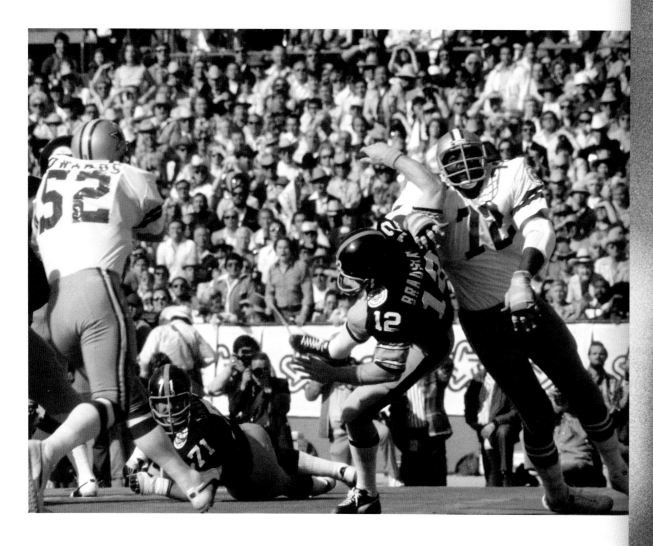

X A 6-foot-9 giant, defensive end Ed "Too Tall" Jones (number 72) menaced opposing quarterbacks for 15 seasons wearing Cowboys blue.

stand as the longest touchdown from scrimmage in NFL history.

On the other side of the ball, the Cowboys of the late '70s boasted the "Doomsday Defense." Led by a ferocious trio of veteran linemen—Randy White, Harvey Martin, and Ed "Too Tall" Jones—Doomsday was capable of devastating opposing offenses. After compiling a 12–2 record in 1977 and giving up only 13 combined points in 2 playoff games, the Cowboys cruised into Super Bowl XII, where they faced former Cowboys quarterback Craig Morton and the Denver Broncos. In the first-ever indoor Super Bowl, which was

TOM LANDRY

COACH
COWBOYS SEASONS: 1960-88

Beginning with his days of playing defensive back for the New York Giants in the 1950s, Tom Landry treated football as a science. He tirelessly studied film, looking for opponents' tendencies, and drew up charts to gain an edge. He became so good at creating and teaching defenses that the Giants made him a defensive player-coach during the 1954 and 1955 seasons. After retiring the next year to become a full-time defensive coach, Landry helped develop the "4-3" defense. Designed to have four linemen up front, three linebackers patrolling the middle, and four defensive backs, it was the basis for Dallas's famed "Doomsday Defense." It became so popular (it was adopted by nearly every other NFL team), that Landry was forced to develop an offensive system to beat it. Landry was also a teacher whose players learned not just about football but about life. "He wasn't just about building football teams," receiver Drew Pearson said. "It was about building men of character. Many of the things he did were to teach us important lessons about our success in life after football."

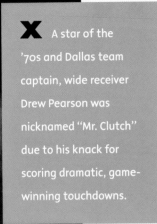

played at the new Louisiana Superdome, the Doomsday Defense forced the Broncos to cough up eight turnovers, including four Morton interceptions, as the Cowboys throttled the Broncos 27–10. Martin and White took home another league-first: the big game's co-MVP honors.

After another tremendous season in 1978, the Cowboys lost Super Bowl XIII to the Steelers. Dallas was then bounced from the playoffs in each of the next four years. Although three of those losses (1980, 1981, and 1982) came in the NFC Championship Game, it was clear that Dallas's supremacy was declining. Then, in 1983, nine Cowboys greats of the 1970s and early '80s announced their retirement, draining the team of talent. Dallas went into the 1984 season without such standouts as tight end Billy Joe Dupree and wide receiver Drew Pearson.

Those departures opened the door for some new Cowboys heroes to step forward. Cornerback Everson Walls and powerful running back Herschel Walker turned in some exciting performances throughout the mid-1980s, but the Cowboys were no longer a powerhouse. From 1986 to 1988, the once-mighty 'Boys posted losing records every year.

A NEW SHERIFF COMES TO TOWN

X- -

On April 18, 1989, a new era in Dallas Cowboys history began

when Arkansas businessman Jerry Jones bought the team.

Jones was determined to turn the proud franchise around.

One of his first moves was to replace the legendary Tom

Landry—Dallas's first and only head coach—with Jimmy

Johnson, the former coach of the 1987 national champion

University of Miami Hurricanes. Despite the controversial

move, Jones was firm in his decision. "History will show that

one of the finest things that ever happened to the Dallas

Cowboys was Jimmy Johnson," Jones declared.

Coach Johnson began rebuilding the team

immediately, making the biggest trade in NFL history by

sending Walker, the team's top star, to the Minnesota

Vikings in 1989 for five players and six draft picks. The team

already had a rising star receiver in Michael Irvin. And with

the accumulated draft picks, Johnson loaded the Cowboys

with young talent, including intelligent quarterback Troy

Aikman (drafted in 1989) and hard-nosed running back

Emmitt Smith (in 1990).

Some experts considered the 5-foot-9 Smith to be too

small and slow for the NFL. But he immediately dispelled

those doubts by rolling up 1,165 total yards and scoring 11

touchdowns in his first season—a performance that earned

X Toughness, sure
hands, and precise
route-running made
Michael Irvin a star; in
1991, he led the NFL in
receiving yards (1,523)
as the Cowboys ended
a five-year playoff
drought.

AMERICA'S TEAM

Success breeds popularity. And in the 1970s, the Cowboys became so successful that their popularity spread far beyond Texas. Bob Ryan, editor-in-chief of NFL Films, came up with the title "America's Team" when he was preparing the Cowboys' 1978 highlight reel. "The Cowboys had just lost a crushing Super Bowl to the Steelers," Ryan explained. "I wanted to come up with a different twist on their team highlight film. I noticed then, and had noticed earlier, that wherever the Cowboys played, you saw people in the stands with Cowboys jerseys and hats and pennants." There's also the "Cowboys Factor" in television programming. "When in doubt, give them [the viewers] the Cowboys," football historian Beano Cook once said. And indeed, since 1966, the Cowboys have been viewed by millions in their annual Thanksgiving Day game. "[It] has helped give us our notoriety," Cowboys safety Bill Bates said. "Everybody is sitting around eating their turkey and watching the team with the star on the helmet. It's a national tradition." A 2007 Harris Poll of football fans confirmed what millions already knew— the Cowboys are America's favorite football team.

him Offensive Rookie of the Year honors. "Sixteen teams passed on me [in the draft]," he said. "I was beginning to think I wouldn't go until the second round. But I hope 16 teams are kicking themselves now."

In 1992, "The Triplets"—Aikman, Irvin, and Smith—accounted for more than 6,500 total yards of offense. With Smith leading the ground attack behind Pro Bowl guard Nate "The Kitchen" Newton, star tight end Jay Novacek hooking up regularly with Aikman through the air, and fiery defensive end Charles Haley leading a rejuvenated defense, the Cowboys quickly rose back to the top of the NFC East.

Behind this collection of talent, the 1992 Cowboys went 13–3 and barreled through the playoffs to meet the Buffalo Bills in Super Bowl XXVII. There, Aikman threw four touchdown passes as the Cowboys crushed the Bills 52–17 to bring home their third world championship.

After the 1993 season, the Cowboys returned to the Super Bowl for a rematch against the Bills. This time, Smith was the star, running for 132 yards and 2 touchdowns to lead his team to a 30–13 victory. The win marked only the sixth time that a team had won back-to-back Super Bowls. It also marked Coach Johnson's final game with the Cowboys. Johnson walked away at the team's peak due to friction with the overbearing Jones.

AMERICA'S SWEETHEARTS

Formed in 1972 by general manager Tex Schramm, the Dallas Cowboys Cheerleaders (DCC) were introduced on the sidelines to add even more entertainment value to Cowboys games. After "America's Team" won its second world championship in 1977, "America's Sweethearts" became pop-culture icons, spawning two highly rated made-for-TV movies in 1979 and 1980. In the decades that followed, the Cheerleaders reached an even higher level of global recognition, becoming an in-demand group for appearances. Since 1979, the DCC Show Group has been involved in the United Service Organizations (USO), which entertains military personnel around the world. The Cheerleaders have made more international USO tours than any other entertainment group. Their annual trips have become such special traditions that the USO gave them the first-ever "Spirit of Hope" award and the distinguished "USO's 50th Anniversary Award." Perhaps even more meaningful, they were inducted into the Veterans of Foreign Wars Hall of Fame in 2002. "They [the cheerleaders] are given a perspective on life that they may not have considered before," DCC leader Kelli McGonagill Finglass said. "And that might lead them to reassess what's truly important ... and to share that with others."

X The Cowboys and 49ers developed a heated rivalry in the early '90s, clashing in the NFC Championship Game for three straight years.

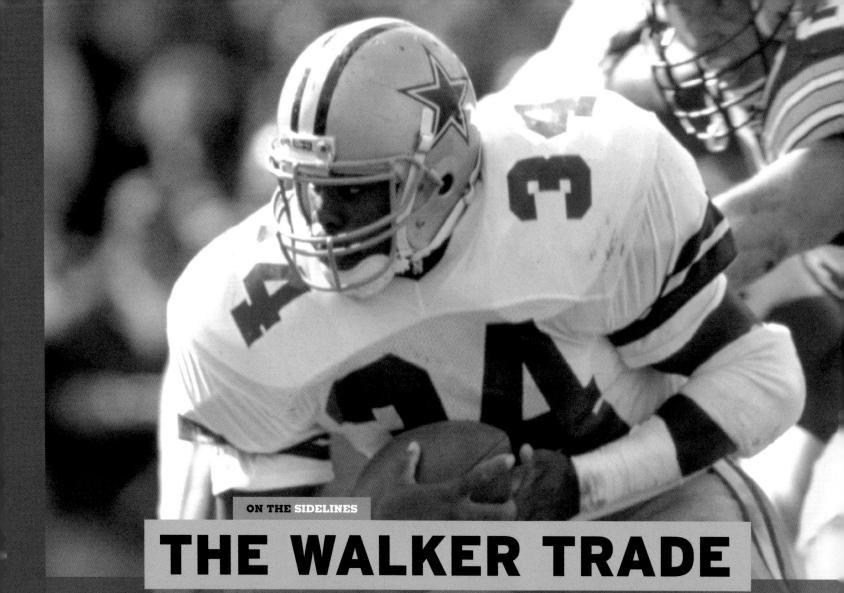

ON THE **SIDELINES**

THE WALKER TRADE

In a deal simply referred to among Cowboys fans as "The Trade," which was agreed upon between Dallas and the Minnesota Vikings in 1989, running back Herschel Walker (pictured) became the centerpiece of the largest player trade in NFL history. In the years that followed, the swap also became widely perceived as the most lopsided—bad for the Vikings but exceptionally good for the Cowboys—of all time. Dallas sent Walker and four draft picks to Minnesota in exchange for six draft picks and five players—linebackers Jesse Solomon and David Howard, cornerback Issiac Holt, running back Darrin Nelson, and defensive end Alex Stewart. Nelson was traded to the San Diego Chargers, and Stewart was waived, but Dallas still got three legitimate players and a bundle of picks to draft even more. Two picks were used to draft running back Emmitt Smith and safety Darren Woodson. Others were used to make even more trades. One such trade led to the drafting of defensive tackle Russell Maryland with the first overall pick in 1991. While Walker never lived up to the massive expectations in Minnesota, he did return to Dallas seven years later to finish out his career.

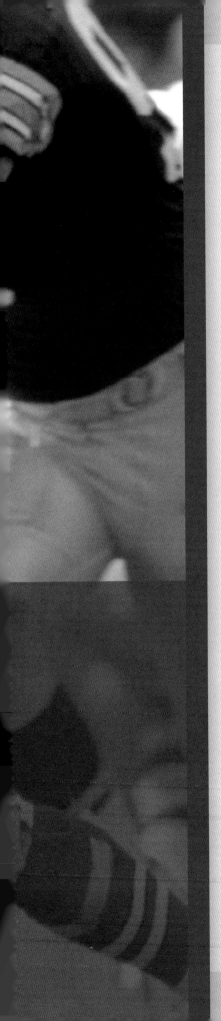

In 1994, former University of Oklahoma coach Barry Switzer took over as head coach of the talented Cowboys. After losing to the San Francisco 49ers in the NFC Championship Game that year, the Cowboys added another big weapon to their already deep roster: Deion Sanders, an incredibly fast cornerback and kick returner nicknamed "Prime Time."

The 1995 Cowboys reached the Super Bowl again, this time meeting the franchise's old nemesis, the Pittsburgh Steelers, the team that had thwarted Dallas in two Super Bowls in the 1970s. Super Bowl XXX marked the first time that two teams had met in the Super Bowl for a third time. And Dallas got some payback, pulling out a 27–17 victory to win its third world championship in four years. This time, the defense dominated, led by tackle Chad Hennings' two sacks and cornerback Larry Brown's two interceptions. "Every time someone counted us out, I looked to my boys on the left and to my boys on the right, and we squeezed a little tighter and pulled a little closer," Irvin said. "The bottom line is that we got it done."

LOOKING FOR A LEADER

x

The Cowboys made the playoffs three more times in the late 1990s. But with each passing season, they became less of a championship threat. The rise of free agency made it harder for teams to keep star players, and Irvin retired in 1999, with Aikman following in 2001. Despite the efforts of players such as star offensive lineman Larry Allen, the Cowboys fell from the playoff picture in the first seasons of the new century. However, one steady presence in Dallas throughout those years was Emmitt Smith. In 2002, the longtime star gained his 16,727th career rushing yard to surpass Chicago Bears great Walter Payton as the NFL's all-time rushing leader.

After going through two new coaches in two years and watching his team go 5–11 in 2002, Jerry Jones made headlines by hiring head coach Bill Parcells, who had previously led the rival New York Giants to two Super Bowl victories and the New England Patriots to a Super Bowl appearance. Parcells was one of the game's most respected coaches, and Jones entrusted him to rebuild the Cowboys.

Whether protecting the quarterback or paving the way for Cowboys running backs, huge (6-foot-7 and 340 pounds) tackle Flozell Adams was a force on the offensive line. **X**

"There will be changes here," the stern and demanding coach promised. "No doubt about that."

Parcells made one of his first big changes before the 2003 season by releasing Smith. Although the move upset many Cowboys fans, it signaled a commitment to building for the future with youth. While Parcells leaned on stalwart veterans such as offensive tackle Flozell Adams, he gave increased responsibility to rising stars such as tight end Jason Witten and hard-hitting safety Roy Williams. By the end of 2003,

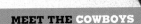

MEET THE COWBOYS

TROY AIKMAN

QUARTERBACK
COWBOYS SEASONS: 1989-2000
HEIGHT: 6-FOOT-4
WEIGHT: 219 POUNDS

In 1989, the Cowboys were struggling badly and needed a new face and leader. Enter University of California, Los Angeles (UCLA) quarterback Troy Aikman, who was selected first overall in that year's NFL Draft. The Cowboys pinned their hopes on Aikman with high expectations that he would turn the team around. And while Aikman went winless as a starter his rookie season, he improved each season thereafter. In 1991, he led the Cowboys back into the playoffs as a Wild Card team. After that, it seemed like the only thing Aikman did was win Super Bowls; by the time he retired, he was only the third quarterback in NFL history to lead his team to three Super Bowl victories. And he did it by mastering the basics of the position. "In my opinion, he's fundamentally the best quarterback that's ever played the game," former Tampa Bay Buccaneers quarterback Trent Dilfer said. "He's perfect. You cannot find a flaw in his mechanics, drop, his throwing motion, balance, all that stuff. Nobody's close to him fundamentally." By 2008, Aikman remained the winningest NFL quarterback in any decade, with 90 regular-season wins, and held virtually every Cowboys passing record.

BIGGER AND BETTER

They say that everything is bigger in Texas. For Cowboys owner Jerry Jones and his design team, bigger means the new Dallas Cowboys stadium, the largest state-of-the-art stadium in the league. Set to open in Arlington in 2009, the stadium was slated to hold up to 100,000 fans and cover 2.3 million square feet, making it the largest domed structure in the world. Built on twin arches that are twice as long as the famous St. Louis Gateway Arch, the stadium could fit the entire Statue of Liberty inside, even with its retractable roof closed. One of the stadium's most innovative designs was a center-hung video board that gave fans sitting in the upper decks a larger-than-life view of the game. "The challenge for us with this new stadium was to innovate, but at the same time never forget to acknowledge tradition," Jones said. Like the original Texas Stadium, the new stadium was designed to include a distinctive "hole in the roof" when the retractable dome roof was left open. Dallas was scheduled to showcase the new stadium by hosting Super Bowl XLV in 2011.

Dallas was 10–6 and back in the playoffs.

After Dallas took a step backward in 2004 with a losing record, Parcells brought in veteran quarterback Drew Bledsoe to help right the ship. Bledsoe worked with such receivers as Terry Glenn and Terrell Owens to push the Cowboys to a winning season in 2005 and the playoffs in 2006. But that would be as far as Coach Parcells would take Dallas. After the Cowboys suffered a heartbreaking, one-point loss to the Seattle Seahawks in the playoffs with young quarterback Tony Romo at the helm, Parcells retired.

Parcells's successor, Wade Philips, inherited a dangerous offense and an aggressive defense that took the Cowboys to a 13–3 record. Romo, Owens, and rugged running back Marion Barber III put plenty of points on the scoreboard, while the defense—led by fast-rising star DeMarcus Ware, a pass-rushing linebacker—was again flexing its muscle.

Unfortunately, Dallas suffered a bitter playoff loss to the eventual Super Bowl champion New York Giants, then underachieved the next season. Although many experts considered the 2008 Cowboys to be the most talent-laden team in the NFC, especially after they started the year 3–0, Dallas began struggling after Romo was sidelined with a broken finger. The Cowboys rebounded enough to post a

EMMITT SMITH

RUNNING BACK
COWBOYS SEASONS: 1990-2002
HEIGHT: 5-FOOT-9
WEIGHT: 220 POUNDS

The knock on Emmitt Smith when he left college for the NFL was that he was too small and too slow to excel as a pro. But Smith had a different game than most other running backs. He maximized his other strengths—smarts, power, and agility—and deployed an explosive burst to hit every hole hard. Lacking breakaway speed, Smith patiently allowed his blockers to open holes for him. And despite his smaller size, Smith was a relentless rusher who had a nose for the end zone. "When Emmitt gets to the goal line," Dallas fullback Tommie Agee said, "he's like a pit bull on a sirloin steak." Smith impressed even his on-field teammates, who would sometimes get distracted when he carried the ball. "One of the biggest mistakes I used to make was just watching him after I handed him the ball, instead of continuing the fake," said quarterback Troy Aikman. "He's amazing." This unique blend of talent enabled Smith to become the fourth player in history to win three straight NFL rushing titles (1991, 1992, and 1993) and become the league's all-time rushing leader in 2002.

winning record, but they finished far behind the Giants in the tough NFC East and missed the playoffs.

The Dallas Cowboys have a history of success that is the envy of most teams in the NFL. In a little more than 4 decades, the 'Boys have won 5 Super Bowls, appeared in 14 NFC Championship Games, and featured some of the brightest stars in the history of pro football. As a new generation of players now don the helmets with the lone star, "America's Team" hopes to soon become America's champs once again.

X By 2008, ferocious linebacker DeMarcus Ware was regarded as one of the premier defensive players in the NFL.

INDEX